TEACH ME TO Pray

TRUE STORIES OF INCREDIBLE ANSWERS TO PRAYER

ANNIE RIESS
ILLUSTRATED BY FEMI AJAYI

This book belongs to:

_____

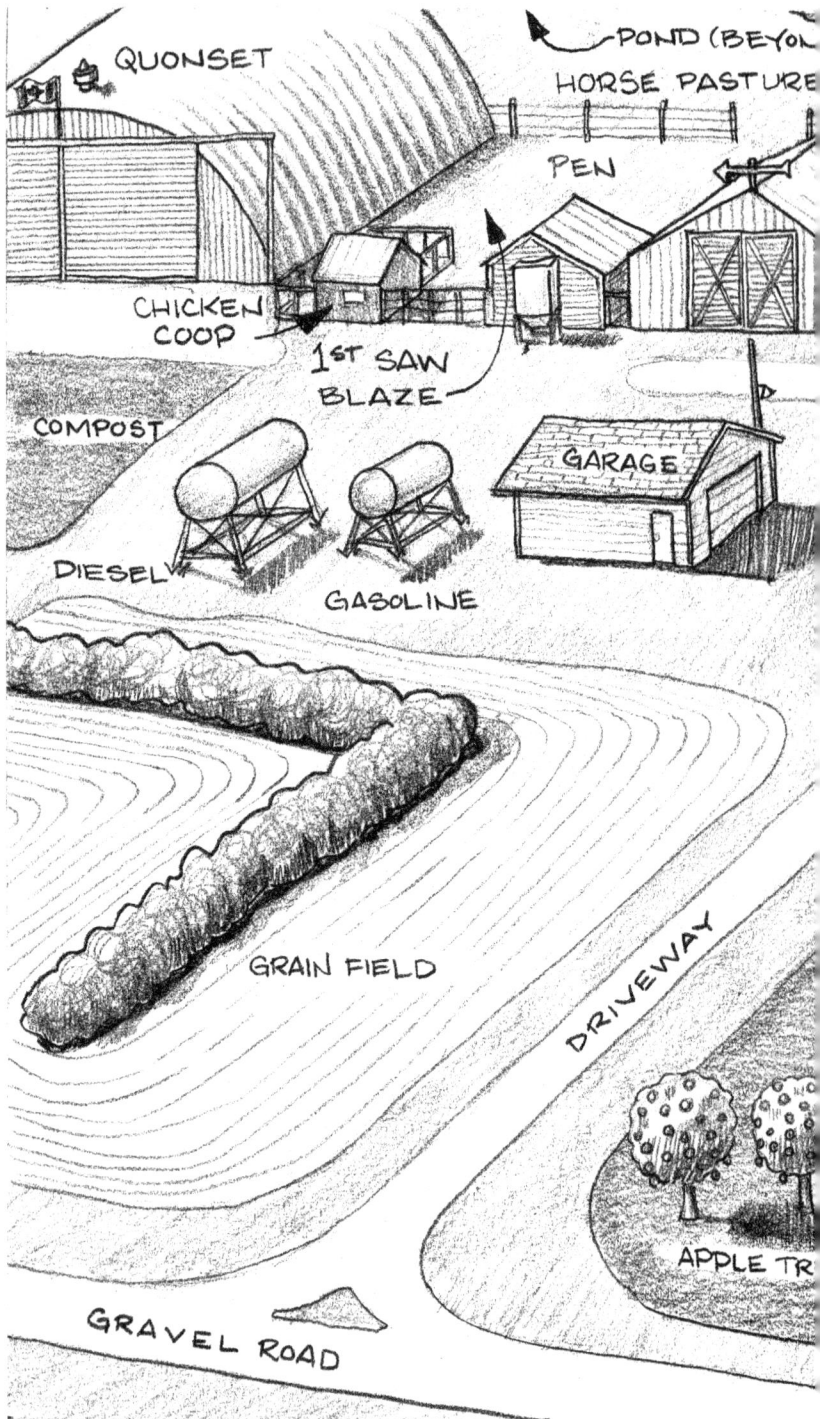

GRAIN BINS

HOUSE

PLAY YARD

GARDEN

SKATING RINK

This book is dedicated to:

Our children: Ryan, Janelle, and Sheldon,
who have shared their stories
on prayer for this book.

And to our grandchildren,
for whom this book was written:
Levi
Annie
Caleb
Ezra
Eden
Connor
Phoebe
Simon
Harvest

Contents

Acknowledgements

To my parents, who taught me to pray.

To the late Dennis Ramsay and Trudy Ramsay, my pastor and his wife through many of my growing up years. They taught me to believe in a prayer-answering God.

To my sister Thelma, who helped and encouraged me through my first writings.

To my husband Ken, who has supported and helped me through living these stories and now the writing of this book.

Dear Parents and Grandparents

What if you could teach your children one thing that would dramatically change their lives and give them hope for the future? I believe that one thing would be prayer. This book of true stories of answered prayers, taken from our family's prayer journal, will inspire you and your child to pray and trust God to answer in His often-astonishing ways.

From stories in Scripture, we get the idea that Elijah was remarkable. Yet we are told, *"Elijah was a man just like us"* (James 5:17, EHV). What made him remarkable? The answer is that he prayed. Prayer gives us hope, because it teaches us to rely on God.

When my husband and I found out we were expecting our first baby, I was very concerned that we wouldn't be able to meet the needs of a child since our income was well below the poverty line.

Yet, throughout my devotions, I kept reading verses such as these:

> Don't worry about anything; instead, pray about everything; tell God your needs… (Philippians 4:6, TLB)

> …do not worry about your life, what you will eat or drink; or about your body, what you will wear… your heavenly Father knows that you need them. But seek first his kingdom and his righteousness, and all these things will be given to you as well. (Matthew 6:25, 32–33, NIV)

I felt God was saying, "Seek Me. Trust Me." I began to seek God and trust Him for each need. Over the years, He has supplied our children with everything from diapers to a university education.

Children have such remarkable faith. They so easily believe for the impossible. Christ said, *"Let the little children come to me, and do not hinder them…"* (Luke 18:16, EHV) Sometimes we hinder them by discouraging them from prayer because we think God might not answer. We must remember that we serve a big God. He will decide when and how prayers are answered.

We received many answers to prayer, but I also want to make it clear that God, like any good Father, doesn't always give us exactly what we want. He knows best. Some prayers aren't answered the way we want them to be, and others not at all. God does want us to ask, though, and often He answers us in surprising ways. Our hope and trust must always be in God alone, not in what we can receive from Him.

Jeff Minick, writing for *The Epoch Times*, says, "Our kids need to be taught hope. Without hope, there is no resilience, no grit to carry us forward; without such tools, we can't expect our young people to find the courage and vision to fulfill their potential."[1]

What could give a child more hope than knowing they have a Heavenly Father who loves them and cares very much about them? I believe these stories from our family's prayer journal will inspire you to believe God loves and cares for each one of us.

> ...we will tell the next generation the praiseworthy deeds of the Lord, his power, and the wonders he has done... Then they would put their trust in God and would not forget his deeds but would keep his commands. (Psalm 78:4, 7, NIV)

May you and your family be encouraged to seek and trust our loving and gracious Father to meet your needs.

---

[1] Jeff Minick, "Strong Foundations Make Strong People: Building Virtue in Our Children," *The Epoch Times*. February 16, 2022 (https://www.theepochtimes.com/bright/strong-foundations-make-strong-people-building-virtue-in-our-children-4274628).

Please Don't Die, Kitty!

"Kitty, kitty, kitty! Come here, Moses," six-year-old Ryan called to his favorite kitten. "I want to see you before we leave."

Ryan picked up Moses with his black fur and sparkling eyes. He held him close and stroked his soft fur.

"We're going to be gone all day, Moses, but I'll see you tonight."

He set his kitten back in the kitten box in the barn and joined his family in the car. They were on their way.

Ryan lived with his family on a farm. He loved the animals and spent hours outside playing with them every day. He had a dog and several red chickens. He had tamed one of the chickens and taught it to jump up and take grass out of his hand. He also had a mother cat with two kittens.

Moses, the smallest kitten, was his favorite of all his pets, and he couldn't wait to see him again.

While they were gone, big black clouds came up on the horizon. The wind blew strong. It wasn't long before they heard thunder.

"Do you think my kitten will be afraid of that loud noise, Dad?" Ryan asked.

"No, Moses is with his mother," Dad replied. "He won't be afraid."

The thunder and lightning continued most of the way home and rain ran down the windows like little rivers. Ryan was glad he was safe with his mom and dad and he hoped that Moses was safe too.

When they arrived home, Ryan sprang from the car and ran through the rain to the barn. He couldn't wait to see Moses.

"Kitty, kitty," he called, looking all around the barn.

But he could not find Moses.

Ryan hurried to the house. "Mom, Dad, help! Moses isn't in his box. I can't find him. Please come and help!

Mom and Dad followed Ryan to the barn. They looked in the mangers, up in the rafters, and behind the feed bags and pails. They couldn't find Moses either.

"He's got to be here somewhere," Mom said.

"Let's get a flashlight and see if we can find him," Dad suggested. "He must've got lost in the rainstorm and can't find his way back."

Dad used a flashlight to shine all around the barn, but Moses wasn't there.

They went outside. Moses wasn't there.

Ryan continued to call. "Kitty, kitty, kitty…"

But they could not find Moses.

Ryan saw that the mother cat had come out and was pacing back and forth. He watched her stop and sniff a lump of dirt in a hole where the rain had run down the eavestrough. It had come down so hard that it had filled the little hollow with water.

Dad noticed the mother cat too and knew that the lump of dirt didn't belong there. He went to investigate.

"Look! I found Moses!" he called, plucking a soaking wet kitten out of the shallow puddle. He held him up by the fur on the back of his neck. "It looks like he's dead. He must've drowned when the rain came gushing down the eavestrough and filled that puddle. Poor little kitten."

Ryan dashed over to see his favorite kitten. He reached out his hand and touched Moses's cold wet fur. "Oh! He's freezing cold. Let's wrap him up in a big blanket and get him warm again."

"That won't help," Dad said. "It looks like he's dead."

"Dead?" Ryan repeated, reaching out to take Moses. "But Dad, can't we shake the water out of him?"

"No, honey," Mom whispered. "Dead means he's just not alive anymore. He can't run and jump or chase the string like he used to. He never will."

"Never?" said Ryan, looking stunned. "But I still want him. I want to hold him."

"Kittens can't swim," Dad explained. "Moses must've lay in that cold water so long he either drowned or the cold killed him."

"Can I hold him?" Ryan asked, again reaching out to take Moses. As he held his kitten, he began to cry softly. "Won't he be all better… if we put him… back in with his mother? Won't she warm him up?" He paused and then blurted out, "We could pray for him… and then can we take him in the house and dry him off?"

Mom and Dad stood there sadly, watching through tears as Ryan prayed over his dead kitten. They looked at each other, unsure about what to do.

Finally, Mom spoke. "It's good that you prayed, Ryan. God always wants us to bring our worries to Him in prayer."

"Can I take Moses into the house?"

"Oh, Ryan, you know I don't like animals in the house," she said. "But just for tonight, you can bring your kitten in. We'll decide what to do with him in the morning."

Ryan carried his precious kitten to the house. Mom found a box and put an old towel on the bottom.

As Ryan laid his lifeless wet Moses on the towel, he heard an odd squeaky noise.

"Mom, did you hear that squeak?" he asked. "Maybe he's not really dead."

"Sometimes when air escapes out of the lungs, even dead animals can make a noise."

Ryan's shoulders slumped. "He's so cold and his fur won't dry. Could we give him a hot water bottle, like you give me when I'm cold?"

"Sure, we'll do that. Then you'll have to get ready for bed. It's getting very late."

Ryan picked up Moses while Mom placed the hot water bottle under the towel. Then he gently laid the kitten back down.

"Mom, could we pray for Moses now?" Ryan asked, raising his eyebrows. "I know God can make him better!"

"Well, honey, your poor kitten is likely not going to make it, but it's always a good idea to pray."

So they did.

"Dear God," Ryan prayed, "please help Moses to get better and be strong and healthy again. Amen."

Ryan put on his pajamas and brushed his teeth. Mom read a story to him and his sister. He fell asleep, sure that God would take care of his kitten.

In the morning, Mom was awake early and thought she heard a noise coming from the kitchen. What could it be?

When she went to check, she saw Moses standing on his hindlegs and looking over the side of the box. His big bright eyes were looking back at her.

Mom scooped up the kitten and hurried to Ryan's bed. She set Moses down as he let out a big loud, *meow-meow!*

Ryan heard the sound and sat up quickly, grinning from ear to ear. He was thrilled to have his kitten back again.

"Oh, Moses, you are the best kitten in the whole wide world!" He held Moses up high above his head. "And God made you all better!"

Moses grew up to be a friendly big cat. He and Ryan enjoyed many adventures together on the farm.

Janelle's Dream to Skate

"Mom! Look at all those beautiful dresses," Janelle exclaimed as she watched the other children at the ice carnival. They were dressed up in costumes and formed lines as they glided across the ice.

Six-year-old Janelle was excited that her parents had brought her. She loved everything about the program, but especially the older girls and their solo performances. They had glided so gracefully, twirling around and skating backwards at times. It looked like so much fun.

On the way home in the car, Janelle decided to ask her parents if she could take skating lessons too. "Hey Mom, can I take figure skating lessons next winter?"

"Oh, Janelle, I don't see how that would work. We live so far from town. With your dad working in town, it just wouldn't work out."

Janelle sat quietly, thinking about how far away next winter was. Maybe her parents would change their minds by then.

When spring came, the meltwater flowed through their yard. Janelle and her brothers took little toy boats and put them in the water to watch them float. They also played in the sand pile and rode their bikes. They made forts in trees and played catch in the yard. In fact, there was so much to do that the summer went by quickly. Before long, winter came around once again.

One evening at supper, Janelle asked, "Will I be able to take skating lessons this year?"

"That wouldn't work with my job," Dad said matter-of-factly.

Mom noticed the sad look on Janelle's face. "Oh, honey, we live a very long way from town and Dad needs our car to go back and forth to work. If you were to go into town with him for skating lessons, you'd have to stay for the full nine hours. What would you do all that time?"

"Why couldn't you and I drive in with the car while Dad takes the truck?" Janelle asked.

"Sometimes the temperature dips down low," Mom said. "Our old truck isn't reliable to be out on the winter roads when it's so cold."

"But Mom, I loved the ice carnival and seeing all those other kids gliding around on their skates! I want to be able to do that too."

"Well, maybe next year. We'll see how things work out."

But that night, when Janelle was in bed, she began to pray. She asked God to help her learn how to figure skate.

That winter, Janelle practiced skating on her own every chance she got. She pretended to spin around like the kids she had watched at the carnival, but mostly she ended up falling. A couple of times when Dad was working, and the family was in town, Janelle went to the rink to watch the figure skaters practicing. Janelle carefully watched what they were doing so she could try the move later.

Janelle liked to toboggan down the hills and make snowmen and build snow forts. She was beginning to think that winter wasn't all that bad after all. If only she could learn how to skate like the figure skaters.

Another summer came and went, and with it all the fun activities of warmer weather. Janelle loved to swim and she also liked to ride her bike and play soccer. But Janelle kept thinking about learning to figure skate and how much fun that would be. She sure hoped she would be able to take lessons the next winter.

When the harvest came and her parents were busy getting the crop into the bins, she started to pray again. "Dear God, I know You are busy, but could You please make it possible for me to take figure-skating lessons?"

The days were getting shorter and the leaves falling off the trees. A few snowflakes tumbled down some days and Janelle couldn't stop thinking about figure skating. She knew it wouldn't be long until the lessons started again.

"Dad, are you going to be working in town again this winter," Janelle asked one evening.

"Yes, I will be. I know that's not the answer you hoped for, but we do need the extra income to be able to put food on our table and gas in our car."

Janelle had a little piggybank of money and decided to ask her mom to find out how much it would cost to take figure skating lessons.

"Janelle, it costs a lot more than we can afford," she said. "And then you would also need a skating pass for the year. Because of Dad's schedule, you would often have to miss your lesson day."

Winter came, and with it the figure skating in town started up without Janelle being a part of it. She still prayed about it often, but she had to admit that the situation certainly looked hopeless. She had to face it: she would not be able to be a figure skater.

A few weeks later, a neighbor lady phoned with an odd request.

"My teenage daughter is teaching figure skating lessons in a village not far from here," she said to Mom. "She needs one more student to fill her class. She would be happy to pick Janelle up each Saturday at 8:30 and have her home again shortly after noon. Do you think Janelle would like to fill that spot?"

Mom was surprised but was quick to reply. "I'm sure she'll be thrilled to take that spot. I'll talk to her about it."

Janelle *was* thrilled. She couldn't believe that her dream was finally coming true. Each Saturday morning, she was overjoyed to get up early and go to the arena to learn how to figure skate.

Since Janelle had the entire morning to take lessons and then practice while others took their lessons, she quickly caught up to the other girls who had been taking classes much longer. She learned how to jump, lift, and spin gracefully. She loved the feeling of gliding around the ice frontwards and backwards, and even stopping when and where she wanted to without falling! She learned how to make patterns on the ice, too. It was so much fun.

It was also a lot of work. Like with anything, it took hours and hours of work to learn how to skate well.

One night as Janelle said her prayers, her mom was surprised to hear her pray: "Dear God, thank You for the miracle You performed to make a way for me to take figure skating lessons. It is a lot of work and not as much fun as I thought. Next year, you won't have to get me lessons again."

At the end of the winter, Janelle had received three badges and a medal, and she was happy that God had answered her prayers.

TEACH ME TO
Pray

A Miracle Rink[2]

"Wow! That snow is just like it is in the big mountains, isn't it, Mom?" eight-year-old Ryan asked as he stood looking out the kitchen window at the snowbanks.

"It sure is, Ryan," Mom replied as she dropped cookies onto a baking sheet. "Do you like winter?"

"Oh, I like winter, but…"

Mom bent to place the cookies in the oven. "But what?"

"Well, I wish I could skate more. Skating makes me feel strong and free as I glide around." He held his arm out and made a gliding motion. "Winter would be so much fun if I could go skating every day!"

"It would be nice. But with Dad working full-time in town, we live much too far to make an extra trip to town."

Ryan nodded. "I know."

That night, as Ryan was saying his prayers, he had a new idea. After he thanked God for his nice warm home and his dad, mom, sister, and brother, he added one more line: "God, could You please help me to get my own skating rink? You know how I love to skate."

Ryan got up early the next morning. The first thing he did was run and look out the window to see if his skating rink had arrived.

"What are you looking at?" Mom asked.

"Well, I thought maybe God had answered my prayer for a rink."

"Did you think God would send you a rink just like that?" Mom asked, snapping her fingers.

"Yeah, well, sort of," Ryan mumbled. "You know, if God is strong enough to part the sea for the Israelites, I don't see why he can't make a rink."

Mom nodded. "Parting the Red Sea was a necessity, Ryan. God isn't someone who spoils us by giving us everything we want."

"Yes, but I was hoping he would think a rink was a good thing for me."

"You can pray, but sometimes God's answer is 'no' or 'wait.'"

The days went by, and each night Ryan continued to pray for a rink. And every morning, he checked to see if it was there.

When Christmastime drew close, Ryan loved to look at the wrapped parcels under the tree.

Maybe, just maybe, that red-striped one has a pair of new skates, he thought. *My old ones are too small. And maybe God would somehow come up with a rink. It would make a wonderful gift.*

On Christmas morning, Ryan woke up early to check if there was a rink in the yard, just in case that red-striped box had skates in it.

But nothing had changed.

He was still excited to open the striped-box with the big red bow—and yes, it did have a new pair of skates!

The next day, he was thrilled when his dad took him into town to skate. Ryan glided around on the ice. When he went fast, it felt like wind blowing on his face. He loved every minute of it.

That night, he talked to God again about a skating rink. And a few nights later, as he lay in his bed, he overheard his parents talking in hushed tones.

"You know, Ryan has been praying for a rink for weeks now," he heard his mom say.

"We can't stop him from doing that," his dad replied.

Ryan lay quietly, holding his breath and hoping to hear some good news about a rink.

"No, we can't stop him from praying," Mom said. "But isn't there something we can do to make him a rink to skate on?"

"I'm afraid not. I don't have the time or the equipment to haul water to make a rink, and you know that our well isn't deep enough to supply that much water. I also wish we could do something. But sorry, the answer is no. We can't."

Ryan rolled over in bed and moaned. "I guess that leaves it up to You, God. It will have to be a miracle."

As the days went by, Ryan kept on enjoying winter. He went tobogganing and played games in the snow. It was great fun, but he never stopped praying for the skating rink.

In late January, the weather turned unusually warm and the snow began to get very soft and stick together. Ryan had fun rolling a small ball of snow. Each time he rolled it over, it got bigger and bigger. Soon he had three different sizes. His dad helped him stack them to make a giant snowman.

"All we need is a carrot for his nose," Ryan said, laughing.

The weather stayed warm. Ryan and his sister made forts in the snow and enjoyed playing outside every day. The warmer weather melted the big snowbanks and made black dirt show through in the garden. There were even a few puddles of water forming, and some ran together to make a huge pond.

One evening when they came inside from play, Dad met them at the door. "It's going to turn cold again," he warned them. "Be sure to put your shovels and toys away."

So they did.

That night, the temperature dropped and the air got cold once again. Very cold.

The next morning, Ryan went to the window to see what the cold had done to his snowman.

"He still looks the same." He laughed. "But I bet his nose is froze!"

He kept looking around the yard.

"The water in the garden is froze too… and I can see the snowman's shiny reflection. It looks like ice. Wait!" He squealed. "It *is* ice! It looks like a giant skating rink! God sent me my rink!"

Ryan rushed to put on his skates. His brother and sister got their skates on as well. Even Dad and Mom laced up, and soon the entire family went outside to skate on the new rink. The ice shimmered as they glided about in the morning sunlight.

Mom took a picture of them all and later brought out a big pair of boots to mark goalposts. Then they each grabbed a hockey stick and raced to score.

Dad took a swipe at the puck, and Ryan hollered, "He shoots! He scores!"

It was even more fun than he had imagined. They played hockey for hours.

That night when Ryan said his prayers, he knew exactly how to start: "You are so powerful, God. Thank You for sending me a rink of my very own."

God had heard and answered a little boy's prayer.

Ryan and his family enjoyed skating on that miracle rink for five weeks that winter. They lived in that house for many more years and never again had a rink form in their yard. It truly was a miracle rink.

TEACH ME TO
Pray

A Pony from Heaven

"I can't wait to see all the little ponies," Janelle exclaimed, jumping out of the car. She dashed across the rodeo grounds to where the ponies were and reached out to stroke the forehead of the little black one.

Seven-year-old Janelle lived on a farm with her dad and mom. She had a big brother, Ryan, and a baby brother, Sheldon. They shared a dog and four cats, but what Janelle really wanted was a pony to ride.

Whenever the family went for a car ride, their favorite game to play was to try to be the one who spotted the most horses.

Janelle was thrilled when the rodeo had come to town because it had horses and horses and more horses. She liked to ride on the merry-go-round and the little Shetland ponies that went around and around. Riding those little ponies was her favorite thing to do, and today she got to do just that!

The owner of a nearby ranch, Mr. Ramsay, had a suggestion.

"Your children sure enjoy the ponies," the man said to Mom. "Why don't you buy them one?"

Wow! Janelle thought. *What a fantastic idea.*

"Yeah, Mom, can we have a pony?" Janelle begged. "Please! Please! Please!"

"We'll save all our own money," her brother Ryan added. "And we'll look after it."

"Ponies cost a lot of money," Mom answered quickly. "It will take a very long time to save that much."

"But we'll work hard and earn lots and lots of money," Ryan replied.

"We'll have to talk to dad about it first," Mom said.

On the way home, Janelle asked, "Dad, can we buy a pony of our own?"

"Ponies cost a lot of money," he replied. "And even more money to keep them."

"But we'll save our money and work hard to buy it ourselves."

"That could take a long time, maybe even years."

"That'll be all right, Dad," Janelle said. "We'll do anything to have a pony."

Mom and Dad had taught Janelle and her brothers to pray about everything, so they began to pray about getting a pony. They wanted a pony with a baby foal. They prayed every night, and every night they asked God to help them buy a pony with a foal.

Their neighbors had horses. Whenever the older neighbor girls came over with their horses, the kids dashed out of the house to get a ride. It was so thrilling to gallop across the field as fast as they could go. Whenever they rode, Janelle dreamed about the day she'd have her own pony.

For two long years, Janelle and her brothers collected pop bottles and sold them. They found extra jobs to do and saved all the money they received for birthdays and Christmas gifts, placing the money in an old tin.

Their savings slowly added up and soon they almost had enough for a pony. Mom helped them read the newspaper ads and watch the "for sale" signs they saw along the highway.

Early that spring, their neighbor's horses had foals. They were thrilled the day Dad drove them over to see the new foals. The animals were sleeping when the kids got there, but they stood up on their long gangly legs and stretched themselves.

Then they galloped up and down the pasture, stopping only a few times to explore something that caught their eye. They chased each other with their tails in the air and then skidded to a stop. It was so much fun to watch.

This caused Ryan and Janelle to want a pony with a foal all the more.

They continued to check out ponies for sale but were disappointed to find out that the ponies with a foal cost a lot more money than they had been able to save.

One night, Mom came to talk to them.

"You know, kids," she said, "God does answer prayer, but not always exactly the way we want him to. Sometimes God has other plans for us, and we just have to trust that He knows what's best for us."

"You mean we won't be getting a pony?" Ryan asked.

"After all the times we've prayed and prayed… God will say no?" Janelle questioned.

"Well, maybe. We can't just demand our own way," Mom continued. "God always knows what's best for us, even when we don't."

Janelle looked very glum. "But Mom, you know how much we want a pony!"

"Maybe God has a special pony in mind for us," said Ryan, "and we haven't found it because we've only been looking for one with a foal."

"We don't have enough money for both," Mom said. "So should we keep saving or start looking for a pony without a foal?"

"Without a baby?" Janelle exclaimed. "No way!"

But then Ryan spoke softly. "Maybe we can't have them both. Besides, Dad says that a pony is a 'hay burner.' So one might have to be enough."

Janelle sighed. "I guess a pony without a baby will have to do, because I don't want to wait any longer to have a pony to ride."

With that, they decided to look for one pony that would be good for riding.

A few days later, they drove up to Mr. Ramsay's ranch to look for a pony without a foal. They saw a beautiful roan called Strawberry. She was gentle and quiet and not too big for a horse. She was just the kind that Janelle and her brothers were looking for.

"Is Strawberry going to have a baby?" Janelle asked Mr. Ramsay.

"No," he said. "But she will be a good riding horse."

Janelle felt a big lump in her throat. She still wished she could have a horse with a baby.

Together, they decided to buy Strawberry, and on a sunny June day they picked her up and brought her home.

Janelle burst with excitement. Her brothers were thrilled too.

That night, Janelle prayed, "Thank You, God, for Strawberry. Even though she doesn't have a foal, I am so happy to have her!"

Strawberry was so much fun! She was gentle and quiet, a terrific pet. Every day the kids went out to pet Strawberry. She stood there quietly, enjoying all the attention. They braided her mane and used the currycomb to make her coat nice and sleek. Janelle's mom would put the saddle on her so they could ride. Everyone loved Strawberry.

A couple of months later, Janelle and her brothers went out to pet Strawberry only to be surprised to see a baby horse standing right there beside her! His legs were long and shaky, and his coat was wet.

Janelle ran to the house. "Mommy, Mommy! There's a baby horse in the pen with Strawberry. Maybe it's one of the neighbor's."

Mom came racing out to see. Sure enough, Strawberry was standing protectively over her new foal. No doubt about it. This was Strawberry's baby.

Mom was astonished. Just like everyone else, she couldn't believe her eyes.

"This doesn't mean God will always give you just what you want," she reminded them. "You know, sometimes God has a different plan, but He always knows what's best."

"I know." Janelle beamed, her eyes full of excitement. "But I'm sure glad he said yes this time."

When Dad came home that evening, he was stunned when he saw the foal. All he could say was, "Unbelievable! I can't believe it."

The next day, he phoned to tell Mr. Ramsay about the foal.

"I… I don't know how that happened," said Mr. Ramsay. "I guess… miracles still happen…"

And so they do.

Teach Me to Pray

The sun shone brightly on the pasture as three-year-old Sheldon begged his mom, "Come and pway, Mommy, pwease."

"Not right now," Mom replied, shaking her head. "I don't have time just now, Sheldon."

"Pwease, pwease come." He grabbed her hand and tried to pull her away.

"Daddy needs me to help. I can't play."

Everyone in the family was excited, for they had just purchased a horse. Dad and Mom were making a fence to keep the new horse in. Sheldon watched as Mom handed Dad a big, big hammer. It was so big that she could hardly carry it. Dad took it, lifted it high above his head and brought it down again and again as he pounded the post into the ground.

Sheldon could see that Mom did not have time to play, so he wondered around by himself while he waited. He kicked at the ground, loosening a few small stones. He picked them up and threw them into the nearby pond. Ping! Ping! He liked the sound they made as they splashed.

It wasn't too long until Mom called, "Sheldon! I'm ready to play now."

Sheldon came running. He grabbed Mom's hand and led the way through the tall trees. The grass was high and the branches of the trees smacked him in the face, but Sheldon pressed on.

Finally, they came to a small clearing.

"Look, Mom, pway," he said, pointing to a little yellow bench.

Mom recognized it as a place they had sat and prayed the year before. "Aww, that's so nice. You want to pray. I thought you wanted to play."

"Yes, let's pway," Sheldon repeated. So they sat down while Sheldon prayed. "Thank You, God, for this nice field and our new pony. Amen."

"Amen," Mom repeated.

"There, Mom, just like you told me. We can pray anytime, anywhere."

That night before going to bed, Sheldon put on his pajamas. Mom brushed his teeth and took down the big Bible storybook.

"Mom, I like these stories about people in the Bible who prayed. Then they had exciting things happen."

"They sure did, Sheldon," Mom replied. "Which one is your favorite story?"

"I like David, the shepherd. He asked God to help him kill a lion and a bear to keep his sheep safe."

"Yes, David was very brave, wasn't he?"

"I think Samuel was brave too. He had to live so far away from his mom and dad. It must've been really scary when God called 'Samuel! Samuel!' Wouldn't you be afraid if God called to you like that, Mom?"

"Yes, I think I would."

"I would be *really* scared if I heard God say, 'Sheldon! Sheldon!'"

"We never know when God might talk to us," Mom replied. "So we need to be listening."

Each night, Sheldon would listen to these and other stories, and then he would thank God for all the beautiful things He had created. He would tell God how big and strong He was to make all these things, and he'd also pray for his dad and mom, as well as his sister and brother.

Some nights he would pray for something he knew his family was praying about too. He always took time to thank God for all the things he had. He knew that being thankful was an important part of praying.

Sheldon also discovered that Jesus had taught His disciples to pray. It was an excellent prayer, and he decided to memorize it. It was from the book of Matthew in the Bible:

Our Father in heaven,
>   Hallowed be Your name.
>   Your kingdom come.
>   Your will be done
>   On earth as it is in heaven.
>   Give us this day our daily bread.
>   And forgive us our debts,
>   As we forgive our debtors.
>   And do not lead us into temptation,
>   But deliver us from the evil one.
>   For Yours is the kingdom and the power
and the glory forever.
>   Amen.[3]

One day, Sheldon overheard the adults discussing how important it was to "agree together in prayer." That night, he talked to Mom about it.

"Mom, you should listen to my prayer and say 'Yes, Lord' whenever you think it was a good thing I prayed about."

"Okay, I can do that, Sheldon."

---

[3] Matthew 6:9–13.

With Mom helping him to pray, Sheldon felt inspired to pray extra long, and he was able to come up with many more things to pray about.

Sheldon loved to pray wherever he went. He would walk with Mom and sometimes say "Hey, Mom! Let's stop and thank God for this flower" or "Let's thank God for this shiny stone, okay, Mom?"

There were several large rocks at the end of the pathway where they usually walked. Sheldon knew that Mom often stopped there to pray.

"I think we should always come here and sit on those big rocks to pray, right, Mom?"

As he grew older, the number of people Sheldon prayed for grew. His mom helped him make a notebook with pictures of people and things he wanted to pray about. When he prayed at night, he opened his notebook and looked at the images he had pasted there. There were pictures of trees and flowers and colorful sunsets. These helped him to remember to praise God for the beautiful things He had created.

Then he would see the picture of his family and he would thank God for each one.

One day, he watched a special about firefighters on TV. Sheldon remembered that his Uncle Danny was a firefighter.

"Mom, can I have a picture of Uncle Danny? I want to pray for him to be safe fighting big fires!" He stretched his arms out wide.

Mom brought him a picture of Uncle Danny.

"Oh, wow! Mom, it even shows his firetruck! Uncle Danny is sure brave, isn't he?"

And so he added Uncle Danny to his book of prayers.

Sheldon also had a make-believe friend who went everywhere with him. When his big brother and sister were at school and he stayed home alone with Mom, he enjoyed pretending that his little friend was with him. He'd have this friend play with some cars while he played with his trucks and cars. When Sheldon got a snack, he'd share it with his friend. When Mom tucked him in at night, she had to cover his friend too, because Sheldon didn't want his friend to be cold during the night.

One night, Sheldon said his prayers. "Dear God, You have made such a beautiful world. Thank You for the trees to play in. Thank You for the pretty flowers by our house. Thank You for creating dogs. I like our dog. And God, I pray for my friend. Please help him to share his toys with me. I like when he goes everywhere with me. I'm glad he didn't eat any of my candies today."

The next day, Mom talked to him about his prayer.

"You know, Sheldon, God is a busy God," she said. "He loves you and cares about your life, but I don't think it's a good idea to pray for a pretend friend. Somehow it feels like we're wasting God's time when we pray for make-believe things."

So Sheldon decided to leave his imaginary friend out of his prayers. That way, he had more time for real people too.

As Sheldon grew, so did his prayers. He knew to praise God for his wonderful creations and to thank God for all the things God had blessed him with. He understood that it was a good idea to ask God for help when he needed it. He also knew he could pray anytime and anywhere, about anything. What an important lesson to learn!

Do you know all the ways that you can pray too?

Christmas Tree Surprise!

"Mom, can we get a real Christmas tree next year," nine-year-old Janelle asked as she took a decoration off a small silver tree.

"But we've always used this little silver tree," Mom replied. "It's become like part of our family. Christmas wouldn't be the same without it."

"But it's so small! Even I'm taller than it is. Everyone else has a nice big green tree… and they smell so heavenly."

"I'll talk to Dad about it and see what we can do for next year."

The family piled the rest of the Christmas decorations into a big storage tub and put it away for the season.

Janelle began to dream about the big green Christmas tree she hoped they would get the next year. She also decided to pray about getting this big green tree.

The snow melted, and soon the grass turned green and hot summer days followed. Janelle almost forgot about the big green Christmas tree, but occasionally she would remember and pray to remind God how much she wanted it.

When fall came, the weather turned cold. A few snowflakes fell. Janelle realized that Christmas was getting close. She knew that God loved and cared about her, so why wouldn't He be interested in knowing that she still wanted a green tree at Christmas? She began to regularly pray, reminding God about her wish.

"God, You know how much I would like to have a big green tree instead of that little silver one," she said. "Can You please help us to get one?"

Weeks went by and the stores in town began decorating for Christmas. The streets and houses sparkled with lights and decorations. The church had a big beautiful Christmas tree inside and Janelle loved looking at all the twinkling white lights on it, as well as the boughs and branches around the church. It certainly looked like they were ready to celebrate something special!

At home, Janelle saw her mom eventually take out the Christmas decorations.

"Remember what we talked about last year, Mom?" Janelle asked. "Can we have a real Christmas tree this year?"

Mom shook her head. "Oh, honey, real trees cost a lot of money, and we don't have a lot of money to waste. Besides, we still have our little silver tree. Once we get it all put together, it's pretty nice."

Janelle watched as Mom set up the little stable for the Christmas scene. Her Dad had made the stable last Christmas, and Janelle was anxious to see how it looked. She reached carefully into the box and took out several figures.

"Here's Mary and Joseph," she said. "They were Jesus's parents, weren't they, Mom?"

"Yes, they were. They were very special people."

"Why were they special?"

"Because they listened to God," Mom replied. "And then they obeyed Him."

Janelle helped her mom put the nice red tablecloth on the table and the decorations on the windows. It was so much fun!

Next, Mom got out the big red candle and the wreath that encircled it.

"Oh boy, candles! Can we have a candlelight supper tonight?" Janelle asked.

"Sure."

Supper was so much fun as the candlelight danced and made shadows in every corner of the room. Everything looked festive and amazing.

At bedtime, Janelle prayed about the Christmas tree again. When she finished her prayers, she turned to her mom.

"Why haven't you put the little Christmas tree up yet?" Janelle asked. "Are we going to buy a nice big green one?"

Mom looked sad as she replied, "We'll see, Janelle. Let's talk about it tomorrow."

The next day, Janelle dressed in a hurry so she could ask Mom about that tree.

"Mom, are we going to be able to get a big green tree?"

"You know, Janelle, we didn't have a very good crop this year. That means there isn't much money to buy things. Especially things we don't need. It looks like we will have to wait until next year to buy a real Christmas tree."

Janelle was devastated. Tears welled up in her eyes. She so badly wanted a big, real Christmas tree!

She put on her coat and went outside. Maybe that would help her feel better.

As she walked, she thought about all the things she liked about Christmas. There was all the special food, family dinners, and the gifts. She liked all of it, but each part cost money. If her parents didn't have a lot of money this year, something had to go—and it couldn't be the food or gifts!

What could she do? It looked like she would have to forget about a big tree. She bowed her head and prayed.

"Okay, God, You don't have to help me get a tree. The silver one will do."

That afternoon, as Janelle rode on the school bus into their yard, she saw that her dad was talking to two men she didn't recognize. The men were holding onto a *big* green Christmas tree. It looked too big to take inside, so they were trimming off the ends of the big wide branches to make it smaller.

"How do you like your tree?" Dad asked.

"My tree?" Janelle squealed. She couldn't believe it! It was bigger and greener than any tree she had ever seen.

The men finished trimming the branches. They pushed and pulled to get that big tree into the house. It took a long time since the space in the living room was too small. They even had to rearrange the furniture.

When they put the tree in the stand and stood it up straight, it was too tall. It hit the roof! So the men carefully laid it down and cut more off the bottom.

Janelle was in awe. She had never seen such a huge Christmas tree!

Finally, the tree was installed and Janelle and her parents thanked the men who had brought it.

"You are so welcome," they replied. "We wanted to cut down our own tree from the forest. And when we cut ours down, we accidentally broke this one off. We thought, rather than waste the tree, we should bring it home and see if someone could use it. We are more than happy to be able to give it to you. We hope you enjoy it."

"Oh yes, we will!" Janelle replied, smiling widely and waving goodbye.

As she went back into the house, Janelle admired the tree. It really was so big and beautiful.

"I bet those men were so surprised when this tree came crashing down," she said. "They didn't know that God was helping them to bring us a nice big tree."

"That's right, Janelle," Mom said. "Today I had priced out the few trees left in town, and they cost a lot more money than we could afford. If these kind fellows hadn't brought you this tree, I'm afraid we'd be putting up that little silver tree again."

Everyone smiled, happy to experience the new adventure of a real tree. It did smell heavenly!

The next evening, the family had a tree-decorating party with the few ornaments they had.

"I love our big green tree," Janelle said. "Even if there aren't very many decorations, it is really beautiful. I'm so glad God answered my prayer!"

"Yes," replied Mom. "Let's give thanks."

And so they did.

A Friend for Ryan

Ryan slumped at the kitchen table with his head in his hands. He dreaded the thought of starting a new year at a brand-new school.

He loved living on the farm. He liked his chickens, especially the red one who would jump up and take grass out of his hand. He had pet cats. They were always looking for someone to pay attention to them. He would tie an object on the end of a string and pull it around in front of them, and they would chase it. He enjoyed seeing the cats lunge to grab it, and then missing it as he quickly pulled it away.

His dog was his favorite pet. Keya was a loyal friend and went everywhere with him. Ryan would go exploring in the trees behind the yard and wander around for hours with faithful Keya beside him. On warm summer nights, he'd unwrap his sleeping bag and stretch it out on the lawn in front of the house so he could sleep under the stars. He knew he could count on Keya to be right beside him. As he looked up at the twinkling stars, he knew God was with him and he was never alone.

But sometimes at school he felt alone. When he had started Kindergarten, he had quickly made friends with three boys. They soon became best friends and spent every recess and noon hour together. They had so much fun. For birthdays, they always got together to celebrate. Ryan's birthday was in June and he loved when the boys visited. They would go to the pond and catch frogs. The frogs would jump and try to get away. The boys would see who could catch the most as they splashed about in the grassy slough. Sometimes they raced around playing ball or football or tag.

But then his friend Chris moved away and the other two friends were placed in a different class at school. Ryan seldom saw them anymore. He missed them.

The night before school started, his mom came into his bedroom to tuck him in.

He rubbed the back of his neck and asked, "Mom, do you think I'll find a good friend at school this year? When I think about it, I feel sad. No one's been able to take the place of Chris."

"It's a new school and things will be different and very exciting," Mom advised. "You need to befriend other boys, Ryan, and get to know them better. A close friend is just a distant acquaintance until you take the time to get to know him."

"Yes, Mom, I know. Every year I try to be friends with at least a couple of the guys. But we never seem to become close friends."

"Friends are important, Ryan. They help you develop important life skills like getting along with other people, and sharing joys and sorrows. Having friends makes you happier and gives you more self-confidence. You know that God loves you and cares about every part of your life. Why wouldn't He care that you don't have a close friend? Let's pray and ask God to give you at least one close friend, okay?"

So they prayed, asking God to help Ryan find the kind of friend he needed.

Throughout that school year, they continued to pray often, and Ryan did his best to befriend the other boys.

Ryan enjoyed riding on the bus with the neighbor boys, even though they went to a different school and had friends of their own. He continued to pray and asked God to help him find that special friend for when he got to high school.

The following summer, Ryan went to camp and renewed his friendships there. It was great to be able to spend several weeks hanging out with all the other campers. He enjoyed swimming, archery, and all the sports that they played. He made friends with several boys, but he knew he wouldn't be able to see them again once camp was over.

With another school year about to begin, he was still concerned about not having a close friend. He went shopping with his mom to buy all the notebooks, pens, pencils, and other supplies he would need.

And all the while, he kept praying.

A year had passed since he had first asked God for a close friend, and he still didn't have one. He guessed he would have to wait a little longer.

School opened and Ryan couldn't wait to get there and find his new friend. He was certain God would have answered his prayer by now.

But when he arrived, he didn't see anyone who was new. There were just the usual guys he hung out with. They were good guys, but he was disappointed that God hadn't sent the close new friend he had been praying for.

One week went by and then another. Ryan settled in to enjoy the classmates he had.

A couple of weeks later, he went with his family to church. Just as church was starting, he noticed a new family come in. A mother and father led the way with a small boy at their side, and following behind were three older boys. Two of the boys were very much the same size as Ryan. It was difficult to tell who might be the oldest.

"One of those boys might be the answer to your prayers." Mom said, leaning over towards Ryan.

"I sure hope so," he replied.

The oldest of the boys was called Kyle. He was exactly Ryan's age and in the same grade! Ryan was thrilled to have a friend to hang out with. They had so many things in common. They both loved sports and played street hockey for hours whenever they had the opportunity.

That winter, Kyle often came to the farm and they wandered together through the trees, playing with the animals and hunting together. They attended youth group and Sunday school, too. Life became a lot more exciting now that Ryan had a good friend to do things with.

"I'm so glad that God answered my prayers for a close friend," Ryan told his mom one night. "While I was waiting, I sometimes wondered if God had really heard my prayer. But of course He did! I just had to learn to wait. Isn't it exciting how God answers our prayers?"

"It sure is," Mom replied. "It sure is."

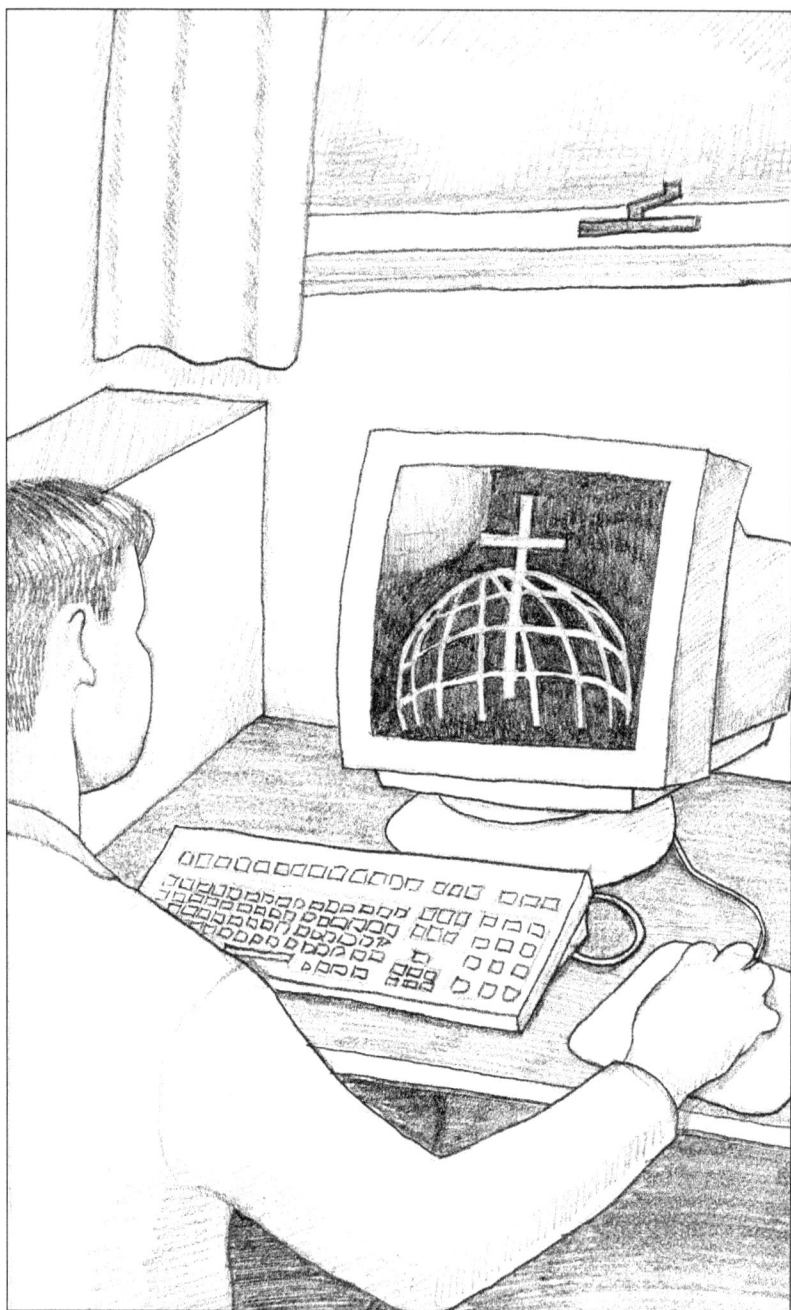

Computer Wanted

"I think I must be the only one in my class at school who doesn't have a computer at home," Ryan told Mom. "I know we don't have a lot of money to buy all the extras, but I think having a computer is a necessity now. There is so much to learn on the computer. We could learn to type, make spreadsheets, and do all kinds of things with it."

"I know, I'm so sorry that Uncle Jim won't be able to get us a good used one like we had planned," Mom replied. "We thought we had a quick and easy answer to our prayers. Computers cost a lot of money, but we'll see what we can do about it."

"Since God has answered so many of our prayers about other things, do you think it would be too much to ask Him for a computer?"

"Remember, it doesn't hurt to ask, but that doesn't mean God will give you whatever you want. Sometimes His answer will be no or wait." She gave him a smile. "And he always expects us to do what we can."

"Well, I think God would agree with me that we need a computer," Ryan replied firmly.

"Yes, I think owning a computer has become a necessity these days, Ryan. Let's talk to Dad and get a feeling for what he thinks."

At supper, Mom brought up the topic of a computer. Ryan's sister and brother were both enthusiastic about owning a computer. Dad also thought it might be a good idea, but he reminded them that computers cost a lot of money. Money they did not have.

"We could pray for one," Ryan said. "Remember how we prayed for the horse? We also saved our money from birthdays and Christmas and from anywhere else we could find."

That evening, they got ready for bed and said their prayers.

Mom closed off the prayer time: "Dear God, thank You for all the wonderful things You have blessed us with. If it is Your will, I ask You to help us buy a computer. Please guide us to one we can afford. Show us the way. Amen."

Then Mom stood up.

"I have some money to contribute toward a computer," she said. "I'll open up a special bank account tomorrow and we'll do what we can to save enough money to buy one."

Life was busy and the kids saved their Christmas money and the few dollars they earned for doing extra chores and collecting bottles. But it didn't seem to be adding up very quickly.

In the spring, Mom announced, "One way we could make money this summer is by joining the local farmer's market. We'd start by planting an extra-large garden. That would mean lots of work, weeding and harvesting the vegetables. Then we'd have to wash them and bag them to make them look nice. We could also sell some jams and baking goods. Do you think that would be a good idea?"

"It does sound like a lot of work," Ryan replied. "But I guess if we want to get a computer, we have to do our part."

Janelle nodded. "Sure, we can do that. I like to bake anyway."

So they planted a huge garden with lots of potatoes as well as other vegetables. It was a lot of work. It was even more work than they thought! They had to spend hours just keeping the weeds down.

Finally, when the vegetables were ready to be harvested, they worked hard digging up the carrots and potatoes. They scrubbed and scrubbed to clean and prepare them for sale.

Each week they started baking cookies and marking the packages on Wednesday. On Thursday, they baked more and packaged more. On Friday morning, Mom baked bread and buns. Everyone helped to package and list the ingredients on the bags so they could be sold at the farmer's market the next day.

"Wow! Gardening and baking is a lot of work," Ryan said with a sigh. "I sure hope a computer is worth it."

"Try not to think about the work," Janelle suggested. "Just think about how much fun it will be to have our own computer."

"But this is so much work and we hardly make any money," he said. "We'd better keep on praying for that computer. This farmer's market isn't a good way to make money. We'll be graduated and gone before we have enough money for a computer!"

Sheldon looked confused. "I'm still praying every day. Aren't you?"

"I sure am," Mom replied. "I want you kids to have a computer. Although it does look like this farmer's market isn't a good way to make the amount of money we'll need."

"This is so disappointing," Sheldon murmured. "I thought we'd make lots of money."

"I did too!" Janelle exclaimed. "We need to pray for a better job."

So they began to ask God for a better way to make money.

Sometime later, they received a phone call from town. It was the man in charge of cleaning up ditches.

"We need miles of ditches picked. There's a lot of garbage out there," the man told Mom. "I know your youth group at the church has helped, but we still need more workers to finish the job. Do you know of anyone who would take this on? It is a grueling job and will take a lot of time, but we need to get this mess cleaned up. It simply needs to be done."

Mom hesitated a moment. "I'll see what I can do. Could I phone you back?"

She hung up the phone and called the kids together.

"We have another opportunity to make a little more money," she explained. "It will be hard work and take several days to pick garbage out of the ditches, but I think it would help us reach our goal. What do you think? Are you willing to do the hard work?"

"Oh, Mom!" Janelle let out a moan. "When we did it with youth group, it was exhausting. Trudging up and down ditches, picking up old diapers and garbage… I don't know if I can do that again!"

"Me either," Ryan lamented. "My legs and back get sore just thinking about it. But I guess if we can get paid lots, that would be a good way to make some more money."

So on Saturdays and evenings, they slogged miles and miles through tall grass along the highways and picked up all kinds of trash, pop cans, and other garbage people had thrown out of their vehicles.

"Who would ever throw stuff out of their car?" Sheldon grumbled.

"People who have never had to pick it up," Ryan snapped.

Janelle scowled. "Well, I think everyone should have to do this for one day of their life. Then they would never throw anything out again."

When fall came, they checked how much money was in their bank account.

"You know," Mom said, "I think we might have enough for a computer. Let's check out what's on sale these days."

They found a computer that cost even a little less than their savings.

"Wow! We'll even have money left over for ourselves," Sheldon said excitedly.

"Not really," Mom corrected. "There are taxes to pay on the computer, and I think you would be much happier with the computer if you had a printer with it. I believe we have just enough money for both."

A few days later, they went into town and bought the computer. It was so exciting to take it out of the big box and set it up.

"Now, was this an answer to prayer, or does it mean we did it all by ourselves?" Sheldon asked.

"Well, I think it was a bit of both," Janelle decided. "We asked God for help, but we also did what we could to earn it."

"That's right!" Mom affirmed. "We did pray and asked God for His help. He provided us with jobs to make money, and a good sale price for the computer. I believe God always wants us to ask for His help, but He also expects us to do what we can."

"Either way, I'm sure thankful to finally have a computer," Ryan said.

"Me too," the others chimed in, smiling.

Janelle held her thumbs up. "Yes, God and us together, we make a great team!"

Cowboy Sheldon

Six-year-old Sheldon reached for his cowboy hat. He was dressed and ready, excited to be going to the rodeo in town. He loved all the action of real cowboys, riding, roping, and even getting bucked off sometimes.

"Mom, I look like a real cowboy, don't I? I have everything I need. See! I have cowboy boots, blue jeans, a belt, a cowboy shirt, a bandana, and my cowboy hat!" He pointed to each item as he spoke.

"Yes, you do look like a real cowboy," Mom replied, helping him into his car seat.

"I like watching the cowboys rope those calves and ride the bucking broncos," Sheldon said, chattering all the way to town. He talked about all the horses, cowboys, calves, and bulls at the rodeo. It was so exciting to him that he could hardly sit still.

Finally, they arrived in town and found a place to watch the parade. They saw lots and lots of colorful floats. The procession was led by a police car and followed by a horse and wagon. There were people on bicycles and people riding horses. Others walked. Some big machinery drove by, as well as little tractors and motorcycles. Banners and balloons filled the air with color.

Sheldon squealed as candy seemed to rain down on him. Having gathered enough to fill his pocket, he scratched open a package of bubble gum and popped it into his mouth. All this candy would last him most of the day.

"Are we going to have a hamburger for lunch?" Sheldon asked as the parade finished.

"We sure are," Dad replied. "Just like we usually do at the rodeo."

Sheldon liked the barbequed hamburger. He piled lots of ketchup and relish on it. "This Is the best burger ever!"

When they were walking around the rodeo grounds, the wind snatched his hat away. He dashed forward to catch it, but the wind carried it out of his reach.

As he dove towards it, he collided with a man going by.

"Oops, sorry!" he said.

He kept going this way and that, trying to get his hat back—and at last, he caught it. He clutched it tightly in his hands.

"I should leave my hat in the car," he said to his mom.

"Good idea," she replied. "You don't want to lose it in that strong wind today."

Later that afternoon, Sheldon and the family climbed and climbed so they could sit up high in the bleachers. The program was going to begin at two o'clock program and they wanted to see everything.

Finally, a group of girls came out riding horses. Each girl held a flag; the first was the Canadian flag and the next was the Saskatchewan flag. Sheldon wasn't sure what all the other flags were for, but he enjoyed seeing the different designs and colors.

A clown was introducing the various acts. Sheldon liked him. He was funny. At one point, the clown announced. "We have a special gift to give to a lucky little cowboy today."

Wow, Sheldon thought. *I'm a little cowboy. Maybe I'll win the prize!*

Near the end of the rodeo, as the cowboys finished riding the bucking broncos, the clown came back out.

"It's time to give away our prize—a two-night stay in a hotel in the city," the clown declared. "This hotel has a golf dome, an exercise room, and a swimming pool."

"Mom, did you hear that?" Sheldon said. "A hotel with a swimming pool!"

Sheldon's family had never gone on a big holiday, but once they had stayed in a hotel. He would sure like to go again, but his parents had told him it cost too much.

"I want to give this to a little boy dressed like a cowboy." Then the clown paused, making sure that he had everyone's attention.

Sheldon's eyes got big as he looked at Mom. Just that morning, he had shown her all his cowboy things.

"Mom, remember? I'm dressed like a cowboy! Right, Mom?" he exclaimed, sliding to a standing position beside her.

"Yes, but other little boys here are dressed like cowboys, too."

The clown continued. "This little cowboy must have cowboy boots, jeans, a belt, a bandana, and a cowboy hat."

Sheldon's eyes got bigger and bigger with each item. It was exactly what he had told his mom that morning… but he didn't have his cowboy hat.

His face fell, and his head dropped.

"Mom!" he cried. "My hat. It's in the car!"

But just then, the kind man sitting behind him took off his cowboy hat and placed it on Sheldon's head. The hat was so big that it came down over his face and covered his eyes.

He tried to take it off, but the man snatched the hat and clamped it back on Sheldon's head. This time Sheldon yanked it off and held it tightly. He didn't want this big hat to blow away like his had.

All the movement in the stands had caught the attention of the clown, who walked over to the fence in front of Sheldon's family.

"Hey, little boy, doesn't that describe you?" the clown asked.

Sheldon put his head down. He didn't know what to say. He really wanted to win that trip to the hotel, but he didn't have his cowboy hat.

The clown once again asked, "Hey, little boy, isn't that you I described? A little boy with jeans, a belt, a checkered shirt, a bandana, and a hat?"

Sheldon just sat, looking down.

Dad answered for him. "He doesn't have his cowboy hat."

"That one will do," the clown said, holding out an envelope with the certificate. "This is your gift, little boy. You just won a stay at a fantastic hotel in the big city!"

Dad reached out to take Sheldon's hand, but he dashed ahead, eager to receive his prize. At the wire fence, he stretched his arm as far as he could to reach the envelope the clown held out for him.

"Thank you!" Sheldon said as he grasped the envelope and hurried back up the bleachers. He was thrilled, grinning from ear to ear. "Now our family can have another holiday in a hotel, Dad. A hotel with a swimming pool!"

On the way home, Sheldon had a question for his mom.

"Why does it feel like God answered my prayer to go to a hotel and swim when I didn't even pray and ask him for that?" he asked.

"Well, Sheldon," Mom replied, "the Bible tells us in James that *"Every good gift and every perfect gift is from above, and comes down from the Father..."*[4] God is a good Father, and sometimes He likes to surprise His children with gifts, just like earthly fathers do."

"Wow! That's cool."

"It sure is," Dad said.

"Whatever reason God gave us this prize, I'm sure glad we got it," Sheldon said. "And I can't wait to go to that hotel. It will be so much fun!

And it was.

---

[4] James 1:17.

TEACH ME TO
Pray

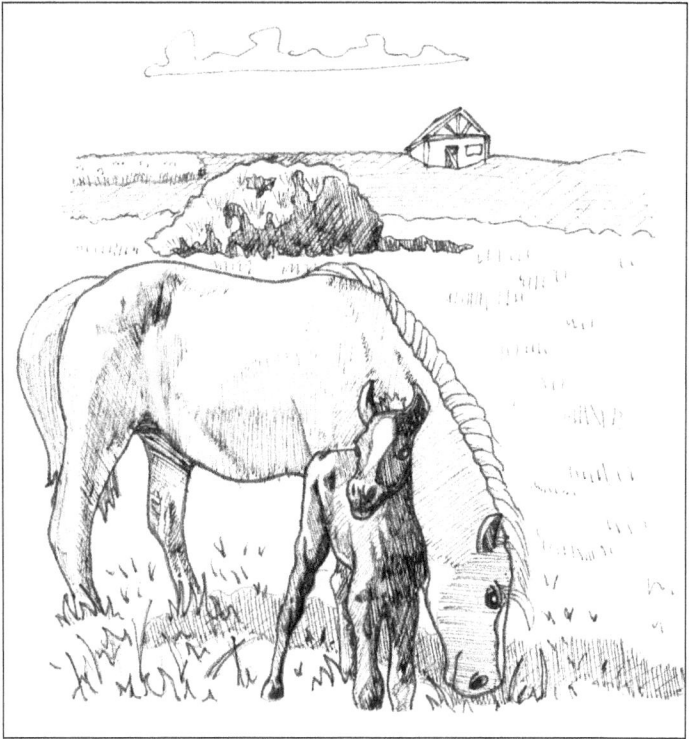

Epilogue

There was a King in the Old Testament, who once said:

> "It is my pleasure to tell you about the miraculous signs and wonders that the Most High God has performed for me. How great are his signs, how mighty his wonders! His kingdom is an eternal kingdom; his dominion endures from generation to generation." Daniel 4:2-3, NIV

It is always a blessing and encouragement to read through our prayer journal, and remember what God has done.

I trust you enjoyed reading the stories chosen for this book. As this book draws to a close, I pray it has strengthened your faith in our gracious God and Father, who loves to give good gifts to his children.

—Annie

writerariess@gmail.com